Having Amazing Relationships

Having Amazing Relationships

Shawn Antonio

ISBN: 1548670774
ISBN 13: 9781548670771
Library of Congress Control Number: 2017915526
CreateSpace Independent Publishing Platform
North Charleston, South Carolina

This book is dedicated to my Unicorn Wife, Alicia and my Rockstar Daughter Viva Jeanne. You are both my FUEL in Life. Thank you for lighting up my Heart.

Introduction

This book is designed to get to the source of how you deal with, view, and function within your relationships. This is an opportunity for you to candidly look at your relationships and how you deal with them. How are you treating your relationships? Let's have an honest look. Is there room for growth and improvement? Let's redefine the relationships that need work.

Each chapter will deal with the specific relationships in your life – with yourself, your parents, your brothers and sisters, your extended family, your kids, your romantic partners, your co-workers and your friends.

It's all about how **YOU** operate within these relationships. This is truly a chance for YOU and what you do in life. A chance to grow, shift, change, take responsibility and expand what's real for you. In other words, time to do some housekeeping in your life.

Do you find yourself having to be a different version of yourself for different circumstances to survive certain relationships? Most people do. More likely than not, you find yourself acting differently with the people you work with than with your parents. I know, because I have in the past.

Let's dig deep and examine who you are in each one of these relationships. Why are you different in each relationship? When did you develop this pattern?

I'm sure if you look at all the relationships in your life, some are great and are working, and some are shitty and need a lot of work. Why is that? The goal is for ALL of your relationships to be AMAZING!!

How you get to having amazing relationships is up to you. It will take some work on your end, to execute the practices in this book. It will involve self-reflection and a willingness to look at your own behaviors and actions. Where have you punished and disrespected yourself and others in your life? You have to hold yourself accountable. All you can do is be responsible for your own actions and words. You aren't responsible for the other person in the relationship. If you accept the other person for who they are, there is freedom. You can only change yourself, not others.

In this book, you will have the opportunity to look at the survival and defense mechanisms you have created within your relationships. If you are being true and honest in **ALL** of your relationships, how would they go? No holding your tongue, just being true to yourself. Acting without filters or fear of 'what could go wrong'. What if you were able to not just survive your relationships and truly be free in them? What if you were able to release your usual triggers? That is freedom!

For example, with my wife there are no filters. There is no holding back, there is only truth and honesty. We have no fear of judgment with each other. We speak candidly and respect one another.

This is possible with all of your relationships.

You also have to consider that if there are people in your life who cannot handle the fully self-expressed version of yourself, then they may no longer have a place in your life. If you withhold your self-expression in your relationships, **YOU** are the one who suffers the impact.

Remember, not all relationships are created equal. You cannot hold every relationship in your life to the same standards. You can't expect your boss to treat you like your friend does. Don't punish yourself or others for the unsaid expectations. This stops you from having amazing relationships. You need to speak your expectations into your relationships so the relationship can actually work.

You have to choose your relationships. You choose how your relationships are going to go. You have to water them like a plant. Relationships take work and commitment to be amazing. Be open and generous of yourself. Be selfless. Be kind, you don't what the other person is dealing with in their life. Take a step back and listen. Take actions consistent with making your relationships work.

A pretty useful tool that I like to use, I call the 'Relationship Tool'. I use three questions to uncover what's missing in my relationships – WHAT, WHY, HOW?

WHAT is the problem?

WHY did it happen?

HOW do you solve or improve the relationship?

Throughout the journey of this book, you will have the chance to apply this tool to all the relationships in your life.

You **CAN** have amazing relationships.

CHAPTER 1
Self

Let's start this journey by looking into how you treat yourself. When you look at yourself in the mirror, what do you see? Do you love yourself, or are you too busy pointing out all your faults? The most important relationship you have in life, is with yourself. **YOU** are one of a kind. There is no-one like you. You were born into this world with a unique set of gifts and talents to contribute to the world. Be authentic with yourself now – are you complete with how you show up in the world? It is important to love yourself exactly how you are and how you're not. Why? Because without self-love, **nothing** works. This behavior completely bleeds into every relationship you have in your life, whether you are present to it or not. Here's the deal – if you don't love yourself, your relationships with others don't stand a fair chance, because you are always going to come from a place of insecurity. A place of needing validation, approval or 'LIKES'. At the end of the day – none of that matters, if **YOU** don't love you. This is the beginning of where you start to fill the voids in your life. Stop filling your voids with empty relationships. Fill it with self-love and acceptance.

I hear you asking – how do I do that?

Let's apply the Relationship tool here. **What** is the upset you have with yourself? **Why** did it become a thing for you – where along the line did this happen? **How** can you get to a place of peace or acceptance about it?

The first step is identifying the parts of yourself that you struggle with. Start by figuring out what those parts are.

Is it physical?
Do you not like your legs?
Do you wish you had straighter hair?
Do you resent your height?
Do you regret 'letting yourself go'?
Is it mental?
Do you think you're dumb?
Do you struggle with letting go of the past?
Do you punish yourself too harshly?
Are you your own worst critic?
Is it emotional?
Are you letting your emotions get in the way of your life?

We allow all these stupid conversations we invented to limit how much we love ourselves. These conversations are the ones where you judge yourself, stop yourself and let past experiences cloud your view of life and consequently get in the way of you taking actions that make your life AWESOME!!!

Why do we do that to ourselves? Shouldn't your relationship with yourself be the most **EPIC** relationship in your life? Shouldn't you love all the things about you that make you stand out?

It's time for **YOU** to love **YOU**. I've learned to live life and accept who I am, and what I am. That's where true inner peace lives.

Now take a few moments to make a list. Write down the things about yourself that get in between you and yourself! Be completely honest about it. Don't hold back! Remember, this is for you and only you. Keep it safe.

***

Now that you have your list, let's uncover some truths!

Looking at your list, you may notice a certain trend. These ideas may or may not belong to you. You have been conditioned by your culture, media, society, family and friends etc. The catch to your list is that it is all things you were **told**, versus the truth about who you are to yourself. You came into this world whole and perfect. Whatever stories you believe to be true, you allow them to become real for you.

Are you **really** too fat? Are you **really** too funny?

By whose standards? Who made up the rules? Your life, your rules. Your adventure.

Don't allow these ideas to put distance in your relationship with yourself. To steal the love you have, for how amazing you truly are. When I say **AMAZING**, I am speaking to **YOU!** Yup, **YOU!**

How does that make you feel? What happened in that moment? Did you have a moment of happiness or upset? That's a pretty clear measure as to your feelings about yourself. If it makes you feel uncomfortable, you need to heal your relationship with self. If you are at peace with it, let's add more **AMAZING** to it.

Now, you need to define where/when/how each one of your listed items took hold of your life. Where did these stories start? Pinpointing exactly where the disconnect originated will be the gateway to self-healing. The **only** way to heal is to recognize it, understand it and accept it.

For example, growing up, I thought I was afraid of heights. This made me feel like I was less than. I felt small and disempowered, like I couldn't do what I saw others do. I thought I wouldn't fit in if I couldn't do the things my friends could do. I used to push myself to jump off of things that scared me to face my fears. I soon realized that wasn't my truth. I wasn't actually afraid of heights. Upon self-reflection, I understood that because adults always told me to 'be careful' I developed a fear of heights that didn't actually belong to me. Understanding that allowed me to feel free and powerful and give me a newfound respect for myself.

So, now – ask yourself those questions. Who told you that you weren't good enough? Who told you that you were different and that wasn't acceptable? Why did you stop loving yourself unconditionally? Why are you judging yourself? There is no need to pick yourself apart. Don't you want to get back to loving yourself?

The key to all of this is acceptance. When you truly accept who you are, and what you are, all that there is, is pure love of self. This is what having an amazing relationship to one's self looks like. I like to think of my imperfections as a life well lived. I celebrate my battle scars. I did the work to dig deep and I got clear that there is only one **me**. This is who I am. Simple. Life is a lot more fun when you love who you are.

If there are things that you don't like about yourself, and you **can** change them – change them! It's your life, and your choices, do what makes **YOU** happy. If there are things you cannot change, you have to create your own way to love **EVERYTHING** about yourself. How can you turn your perceived weaknesses into your strengths? Self-love translates into confidence which makes you magnetic.

Never lose sight of who you truly are. Often there are times we can **allow** relationships in our life to blind us. Sometimes we get lost in them. You should never allow anyone to get in between **you** and yourself. For example, take romantic relationships. Have you ever dated someone who was always putting you down? Criticizing, or judging you? Did they make you doubt or question yourself? This is an example of someone obstructing your connection to self-love. These people can show up anywhere in your life. Practice cutting anyone negative out of your life. Toxic people hinder you from being your true self. We allow them to get in the way of our true self-expression. If that person is someone you cannot remove from your life (i.e. a parent) have a conversation with them. Tell them honestly how you feel and what actions and words affect you. Design anew your relationship. If they still are not committed to growing and stopping negative or critical behaviors, then you have a choice. Moving forward you define how your relationship looks. You decide how you allow them to show up in your life – you call the shots. After all, it is **YOUR** Life.

We condition people to abuse us the way they do. Don't allow it anymore. Stop it today. They get into a pattern of comfort when there are no consequences. It's your fault. When you stop allowing their negativity into your world, you win. You remember who you are without their stories.

Now that you have worked to identify, define and accept the things about you that need healing and self-love, I want you to make another list. Let's call this list, **THE THINGS I LOVE ABOUT MYSELF**. Write down **EVERYTHING** that you love about you. Celebrate yourself. We often forget to be grateful. Gratitude is a huge part of the human experience. When we live in it, everything shows up beautifully. Be present to what you bring to the table and appreciate it. Don't forget the greatness that you are.

I want you to be able to look in the mirror and say – **THIS IS ME**.

When you love yourself, the world loves you back.

CHAPTER 2
Parents

Who are your parents? Is it Mom and Dad? Do you have a single parent? Are you adopted, or in foster care? Are they your Grandparents? Is it Mom and Mom or Dad and Dad? Do you have step-parents? There are so many different kinds of families. Not everyone fits into the traditional idea of 'parents'. Whoever your parents are for you, that's who we are talking about.

They are the first of the influences in your life, the first ones to nurture and guide you. The first ones you fall in love with. We come into this world with pure love. No filters, no bias, just love. Your first years growing up are your most impressionable. All you are is present to life as it happens. So, you look up to your parents for answers and guidance. This is where you develop your trust, where you develop who you are. The relationship you have with your parents is usually the one that defines how the rest of the relationships in your life go. Not always, but usually. We mimic what we see. At a certain point you start questioning their authority, what they are telling you and what you are seeing. At a certain point, you start to steer the boat and create what your relationship is going to look like with each of your parents. Organically, you develop different dynamics with each of your parents. This is the norm. Inherently, you have a different connection with each person in your life, and your parents are no different. You build your relationship muscle with your parents and it extends into your other family members and friendships as you grow and develop. My point is to acknowledge how important those relationships with your parents are in forming the foundation for all other relationships. It is the genesis of how you relate to all others. This is a direct result of what you saw growing up and how your parents treated you. This most important relationship can make or break you. For example, if you grew up with parents who never said 'I love you' you can grow up emotionally shut down. As a result, you can be unemotional and look for validation and approval in others. You likely have no self-love and desperation shows up too. On the other hand, if you have parents who are always open, honest and full of love, you are most likely to be self-expressed and generous in your other relationships. A pretty common theme I've heard often from people is a fear of abandonment. This most often stems from our relationship to our parents. That's just one example.

What shows up for you around your parents?

Be honest. How is your relationship with your parents right now? Are they living? Or deceased? Or absent? You can still have a broken relationship with a parent who is no longer around.

Is it **AMAZING**? Is it average? Or is it broken?

In all my years of coaching people, parental relationships are a trigger for most. That being said, I know a lot of people who have great relationships with their parents. But, there have been breakdowns, resolved or unresolved.

When you hear 'parents' what is your emotional response? What's the first thing that happens to you? Do you cringe? Do you smile? Do you pause? What shows up? Everyone has a different experience in that moment. Take it in. Be with it. Have whatever that feeling is for you – acknowledge the is-ness of it. Right now, that is what's real for you about how you feel about your parents. Let's look at it, instead of running from it. Remember, this is all about plugging into those emotions and not discarding them. If it's anything less than amazing, you need to be responsible for it. Don't place blame. Be accountable for how the relationship has grown or not grown - it's a two way street.. Look at the relationship for what it is and use the relationship tool.

What is the divide?

Why did it happen?

How can it be repaired?

There are always two people in a relationship. You both participate. But all you can be responsible for is your actions – what **you** say and what

you do. You are the source of healing any breakdowns with your parents. I'm not saying it's your fault. But if there is an issue – confront it. Don't let it fester. The point is to have **AMAZING** relationships. Your parents are important in your life.

Somewhere along the way, upsets occur. Promises get broken, resentment builds up, disconnects and communication breakdowns happen. As we grow older, we pull away as we are discovering ourselves and our independence. It's almost as if we all go through this push-pull with our parents. It's natural for this show up in anyone's relationship to their parents. Why does this happen? Unsaid expectations. Lack of communication. Promises broken. Assumptions. Stories we make up. The practice is saying what you want to say, don't hold back. Remember, you only have control over **your** words and actions. Not theirs. However they respond, is up to them. What you can do to grow the relationship is to learn to accept it as it is. Acceptance is key. It will alleviate future upsets. It is cliché, but be the change that you want to see in the world. Be the example. You step your game up. Acknowledge who you are and who you aren't in that relationship. Add fun and play into your relationship with your parents. Shouldn't it be fun? They should be your favorite people in the world, but often times they are not. Understand that they are human too. If you are growing, the idea is that hopefully you will inspire them to grow with you. If they cannot change, create peace for yourself around that. It is what it is. Once you have clarity about who your parents are, it is a lot easier to love them for who they are and who they aren't. That's the truth. We create the context for our relationship with our parents, and they do the same with us. It's automatic. It's who we are as humans. It's called relatedness. So, if your relationship with your parents is not working, then change the context.

The whole point of this chapter is to realize that whoever your parents are for you – they're the only ones you have. One day they won't be around. You don't want to have any regrets or unspoken conversations. Practice having a healthy relationship with them. Be open, love them fully and heal any wounds. Let go of the shit that doesn't matter. We have a finite amount of time on this planet. Don't take the relationship for granted. We all die. That's a definite. Clean up that relationship now. Time keeps moving. When they are gone, it's over. You don't have another chance. I promise you that you will come to regret not having healed any damage. If your parent or parents are already gone, look at the relationship honestly for what it was. Try to understand things from their perspective – step into their shoes. You don't know why they made the choices in life that they did. If your parents are still here, you can always just ask them. Then forgive them and forgive yourself. Just love them.

If you heal the most important relationship in your life, I can guarantee you all of your relationships will get better.

Get in action today.

Don't make an excuse, don't wait for tomorrow – do it now.

CHAPTER 3
Siblings

I f you have brothers or sisters, this chapter is for you. If you are an only
child, this may or may not apply to your life. However, take a moment
to look at what your relationship is to being an only child. Do you have
built up resentments? Do you feel lonely and alone? Do you feel like an
outsider or struggle to be socially comfortable? Are there things that have
shown up for you in the absence of any siblings? How is it for you being
an only child? Just take a look at it – some people may love growing up
being the sole object of their parent's affection and attention, but others
may feel like they missed out on an important relationship in their early
years. Rediscover for yourself how you are about being an only child. If
any feelings of incompletion show up, deal with them now. Have the conversations that need to be handled – with yourself or with your parents.
Grow today. Not tomorrow.

Some questions that may come up for you:

What don't you like about being an only child?

Why is that an issue for you?

How can you create acceptance for yourself?

***

For those of you who did grow up in a full house, let's take a ride on the
sibling rollercoaster! Let's start at the beginning – right now, today. How
are your relationships **currently** with your siblings? Whether it be one, two,
three or more – are they healthy or do they need repair? Commonly, there

are several kinds of dynamics that define sibling relationships all over the world. The family hierarchy always sets the tone for your childhood. Are you an oldest child? Youngest child? Somewhere in the middle? The order of your birth automatically makes you feel a certain way about your place in the family and the world. Your behaviors can be a result of this. Eldest children often feel the need to lead by example and be responsible. The middle children may scream for attention and sometimes feel neglected. Youngest children are often babied and coddled and can feel the need to rebel as well. When your siblings come into your world you grow up together. You develop a comradery and a connection. During childhood, you create a unique bond with each of your siblings that is different from other relationships.

There is a basic format for how your relationship with your siblings go. The sibling dynamic is the same the world over. This pattern transcends race, culture and time. It can look like fighting over toys, vying for attention, acting out, getting each other in trouble, etc. It also is one of love, connection, having adventures together, growing up side by side and learning life lessons as well. Children are fire-starters by nature. They light fires for attention, validation, love, fun and control. It can create tension, chaos, connection or disconnection – it sets the tone and conditioning for the relationship between siblings for the future. Usually. When we condition ourselves to operate based on our childhood, immaturity and stories from our upbringing can take a hold of us.

What comes to mind first for you when you think about your brothers or sisters?

Are there things that are incomplete from your childhood that you haven't dealt with or acknowledged? Are you holding on to any resentments or upsets?

What happened?

Why did you attach meaning to certain actions?

Did they let you down?

Did they break your heart?

Your immediate family often are the first to disappoint you in life. To break promises.

Younger siblings learn by watching their older siblings.

We express ourselves freely as kids. We only start holding back when we are taught to. We stop sharing and speaking our truth because we were shut down, told we were wrong, embarrassed or not heard. Sometimes, we can feel unheard in the family dynamic because of the sibling relationships. Before we can develop anything that holds us back from our self-expression, we may get in trouble for telling the truth. It's something we learn along the way.

What happens is that there are expectations and assumptions. As kids we assume our parents and siblings will keep their promises. Here's what usually happens in relationships in general – we have expectation versus reality. It is the unexpressed expectations that get us in trouble. When we don't vocalize our expectations in relationships, the other person does not stand a chance to fulfill them. Can you think of an example where you have done this?

Our relationship with our siblings is where we build trust, loyalty, companionship – they see the most vulnerable side of ourselves. This can be where problems start. If you don't catch any issues at a young age, they become part of who you are. It becomes an is-ness for you. All these relationships are fundamental to your growth. They help design and create how you live in the outside world. If you have damaged relationships with your brothers and sisters, you inherently create disastrous relationships. If you have positive and uplifting relationships with your siblings, it is empowering. If your relationship to them isn't **AMAZING** and **POWERFUL**, then there is some work to do. Get on the phone and start cleaning up any messes. Or not, it's ultimately up to you. If you want amazing relationships, it takes work and responsibility to heal old hurts. You want to create a path to forgiveness. Forgiveness and letting go is so key to healing. Letting go takes practice. Sometimes the other person (in this case, your family) may or may not want to repair the relationship. So, you also need to learn to accept that for what it is. Take a look at any damaged relationships with siblings and use the relationship tool: **What, Why, How?**

It's not an easy journey to look in the mirror and deal with all your old wounds, but there is power in fixing any trauma that may still be defining your life. It takes humility, patience and digging deep. You have to be willing to want the best relationship available with your brothers and sisters.

CHAPTER 4
Family

Now we are going to get into the people we call family. Uncles, aunts, cousins, grandparents and extended family members. These people play a role in building your community from the get go. This is your first village, per se, of people that impact you in your youth. We automatically relate to them because they are family. Because we are related to them, they are immediately a part of our early inner circle. They can inspire us, guide us, be our examples and teach us about life. On the other hand, for some of us, perhaps we don't get that chance with certain family members. I know some of you may have that weird, awkward or creepy family member that you avoid at holiday gatherings. We all have that aunt or uncle that can be just a bit too much with their over-affection. Or in my case, family you don't really know well from other countries that you aren't particularly close with. Either way, family is family. The impact plays a part in your life.

As we grow up, those relationships may grow, fall apart or circumstance might change it. For example, when I was young, my family and I moved away to another state, away from my family. I haven't seen many of them in over 20 years. However, I have chosen to keep those relationships alive by reaching out and staying in touch. That is a simple choice. Ultimately, it is a two-way street. It is up to you **both** to maintain that relationship. We commonly let distance define how we operate within our relationships – particularly with family. However, some people grow up most of their lives in close vicinity to their family members. Culture can often define how family members live and relate to each other. For example, in many

Mediterranean cultures, families tend to be very close and highly involved in each other's lives. Another example is the Latin-American community, who can frequently live in large family groups.

Now, looking at your own family dynamic, what circumstances define your relationships?

Do you live near or far?

Do you see them often, or just at family gatherings?

Do you keep in touch?

Do you make a choice to see your family members, or do you just 'end up' seeing them?

Do you even like some family members?

Does your cultural upbringing play a part in how family members are involved in your life?

If you remove the title, 'Aunt' 'Uncle' 'Cousin' etc. who is that person to you? Would you have them in your life or not? Most people feel obligated to honor the title, whether or not they actually like, respect, or trust that family member. Does this sound familiar to you?

To give you an example, my wife hasn't spoken with or seen her paternal grandmother in over 20 years. She and her parents made a choice to remove her from their lives when she was a young girl. Whilst it wasn't an easy decision for them to make – they recognized the drama and the trouble that came with having her around. She was the source of a lot of upsets and breakdowns, on purpose. After many years of bad behavior and interfering in the family dynamics, they came to understand that it would be beneficial to cut her out. My wife will openly admit that she never felt like that particular grandmother ever loved her or did anything nice except out of competition or spite or keeping up appearances. As a result, my wife has never missed having her in her life, as her grandmother had never bothered to build a genuine and loving connection with her. In fact, the tensions between other family members were eased by removing the source of the manipulation and stress. Sometimes, this is an important decision to make. Just because someone is related to you, does not mean that you should keep them in your life if they are toxic to you. If you had a splinter in your thumb, you'd remove it. The same should be true for family members that cause pain. When you take away the pain, it opens up your life to AMAZING things.

What do you want your family relationships to look like?

Why are they great or not great right now? How can you fix them or make them amazing?

Do you **want** to make them amazing?

Ask yourself these questions. Are you starting to see a pattern in the relationships in your life?

Apply the relationship tool to the relationships with any family members that could be better.

What, Why, How?

Identify how to improve the relationships that need work, and be honest about the ones that need to go if they exist only out of family obligation.

CHAPTER 5
Love

What do you define as love? What is love to you? When did you learn what love is? This chapter is about **LOVE**. Your relationship to it, and your romantic relationships. Romantic relationships can be complicated. Why? It's because **WE** complicate it. We get attached to an idea, lose ourselves and forget sometimes what really matters. Love is simple. You meet someone, a spark happens. What you do about it, from that moment is up to you. Do you follow it? Do you ignore it? What happens next – is in your hands.

What shows up for you around love? What's your first thought when it comes to love? Be honest. Many of us have a colorful history when it comes to love. Some of us might not. You may be experienced in matters of love, or not. For those who have dated many, I'm sure you can name at least a couple of exes that bring up strong emotions for you. For those who haven't, I am sure your view of love is important to you. So, then how does it affect you in future relationships? You have the opportunity to look at how you deflect and avoid letting love in. This is a **BIG** thing. Many people who come to me for coaching struggle with accepting love. Many of us run from love because of past fears and experiences getting in the way.

I'm not good enough.
I'm not worth it.
I'm not special.
I don't deserve this.
I'm not lovable.
No-one wants me.

I'm ugly.
I'm broken goods.
I'm too needy.
You're too good for me.
I'll ruin it.
I'll fuck this up. Again

See how the past shows up for you, and you allow it to run your life. You need to take ownership of how you live and operate with love. The time is **now**.

We actually give our fears power. What if you didn't put those fears in place? What if you just let love in? How would that experience be for you? If love was just **LOVE** how would it touch you? From my perspective, it would light your heart on fire. **Love is the purest form of energy in the world**. It moves mountains. It's the source of millions of songs around the world. It is the one thing we all **crave** and **want**. So, why do we fight it?

We fight it because, as a general rule, we have allowed ourselves to be conditioned that love just never works out. We watched love as a concept growing up and then we choose how it is going to **BE** for us. We have our first feelings of romantic love at a young age. Remember your first crush? Remember those feelings? Those butterflies? The nervous stuttered speech. The sweat. The awkwardness. Where in your life did you stop allowing yourself to feel that way around love and why? What happened? If you can identify it, you can set yourself free.

Love is **Love**. It's a simple thing. It's a gift.

Let's get really clear about **YOUR** relationship to romantic love. How do you treat it? Like every other relationship in your life, if there is a disconnect – it needs to be healed. On a positive note, you may be one of those whose relationship to love is healthy. Perhaps love has always worked for you, relationships flow and you don't have any breakdowns around the possibility of love.

For myself, I've always viewed love as beautiful, open, gracious, and amazing. So, I've always respected love. The fact that we get the opportunity to meet someone that we can be in love with, in itself, is something special. How cool is that? I am a child of divorce and I've seen a lot of family and friends get divorced. But, I made a choice to not let that define what love is for me.

***

Now, having looked at your relationship to love itself, how does that translate into your current romantic status? Are you single? Married? Divorced? Dating? Widowed? How are you operating? Are you swinging the bat when it comes to love? Are you sitting on the sidelines? Where do you stand? Are you playing it safe or giving of yourself fully?

How are you operating within your current relationship status?

Are you defensive?

Are you loving?

Are you generous?

Are you absent?

Are you present?

Are you committed?

Are you disconnected?

Are you lazy?

Are you being the person your partner fell in love with?

Are you comfortable?

Did you stop playing and having fun?

Are you stagnant?

Are you happy?

Are you complacent?

Are you fun to be around?

Are you looking elsewhere?

Are you honest?

Do you have one foot in and one foot out?

The "grass is greener" conversation can play a part in romantic relationships. We do this thing where we are always looking for the next best thing. We rarely look at what is right in front of us. Being present in your current situation is what makes the difference.

Take inventory of what you really want and if you're not getting that, create it. How you create what you want out of your relationships is to get **CLEAR**. Make a list of what you want and what you need to make you happy in your relationship. There are certain needs that are non-negotiable and there are certain wants you can compromise on. If your relationship has fallen apart, get real about what needs to be done (on both sides) to make it work again. Then, there is a conversation. First, with yourself. Be truthful. Don't hold back. Don't attach yourself to an **IDEA**. Live in the reality about what your relationship is. Good or bad. Then, have a conversation with your partner. Talk about the elephant in the room. If there isn't an elephant in the room, be open about discussing ways to make the relationship better, and more fun, and take it to that next level. Wherever it goes, be accepting of the outcome. Something I commonly practice with my wife, is asking "How are we doing?" I check in because I want to make damn sure that I am fully participating in my relationship, and if not, I want to step my game up and get back to knocking it out of the ballpark. It also grants my wife permission to be honest and open about what she needs in our relationship on a regular basis. I completely recommend this practice. It's a great way to check in and see how are you are treating your relationship. You both need to take responsibility for your actions and commitment. Stay accountable and non-accusatory. Remember, when you first met – there was a honeymoon stage. You were each other's everything. You were addicted to each other and your experience of love was **tangible**. Can you get back to that place? Sure, life throws shit at you. We all get beat up by life. Our relationships bear the weight of that. We hurt the ones we love the most and that is all too common. But, isn't love worth it? Your partner should be the one who stands by your side, the one who is your biggest fan and your most trusted cheerleader. You should have that fire be the source of your inspiration in life. A reminder – if you need a place to start, go back to the relationship tool.

What is the divide?
Why did it happen?
How can it be repaired?

Having said that, if there is doubt or second guessing or not feeling fulfilled in your current relationship, you **need** to deal with it. Spend **NOT ONE SECOND OF YOUR LIFE UNHAPPY.** Look at what's not working, what is not lighting your heart up, where the ball has been dropped and have the uncomfortable conversations. Approach your partner, have a sit down, and talk about what's real. Make a choice – make it **EPIC** or move on. Breakups **can** be easy. You just have to acknowledge what's not working and move on if it can't be fixed. You **can** set each other free with love.

"Thanks for the memories, it was great, but it isn't working now."

"We've grown apart."

LET THEM GO.

Here's the choice in life. You can either have an amazing relationship to LOVE or not. Ultimately, it's always up to you. Stop allowing for anything else to get in the way of that. It's all bullshit.

Remember – **NEVER SETTLE**. For less than what lights your heart ablaze.

CHAPTER 6
Your Kids

Our relationship to our children is very specific and unique. It is truly **AMAZING** that we get the pleasure of raising kids. What a **GIFT**. They remind us to play and have fun in life. They also trigger moments of frustration and challenges in us as parents. Our kids are a reflection of who we are. We are their example – they mimic us as they find their way in the world. They watch us, they learn from us, and then they define who **they** are. We are their guides and they look up to us. When they have questions, we are supposed to have answers. They put us on pedestals and to them, we are invincible.

What's great about having your own children is that it gives you a chance to learn what unconditional love is. To foster intimacy, to break through your own imperfections and to live in pure joy. We get the opportunity to guide our kids into being the most amazing and loving human beings that they can be. Here's where we get a chance to really look at ourselves. Are you being a great example? Are you being present with them?

Your children just need **LOVE**. Are you being that for them? They want your attention, validation and physical connection. Physical connection is a huge part of your child's development. Giving them daily hugs, kisses and touch is essential to their wellbeing and growth. Educating your kids on the basics of life and showing them how to be **AWESOME** people in the world is an invaluable lesson. You have the chance to raise a great human being. Do that.

All that said, that doesn't mean parenting is easy. It's just something new. It will challenge and grow you. You basically choose what rules and structures work for you and your family. You do and be that. Be aware of possible patterns from your own childhood that you bring into your parenting style. Are you bringing your baggage from your past into your parenting? One of the most common fears that comes up for us is becoming like our own parents. Has this happened to you? Have you repeated your past? How can you create your own style of raising your children? Ask yourself what kind of people you would like your kids to be. Not that you have any control over who they become but you can be a stellar example of a person that motivates them to be extraordinary. Are you giving them all that you've got? Or, are you holding back? You might not even know you're holding back but it is worth the inquiry.

It is really important to not carry your baggage from your own childhood (good or bad) into how you guide your children. Remember, it's up to you how you raise your kids. There really isn't a specific way to be a parent. You can do it any way you like as long as it comes from a place of **LOVE**. Like every other relationship in your life, it's a choice. You can be actively involved in the relationship with your kids or not. A lot of people give a 'version' of themselves to their kids. Who can you be for your kids that they feel connected to you? Are you phoning in being a parent?

For me, I purposely developed an intimacy with my daughter, that is separate from my wife. I practice being present, available, loving, generous, kind and attentive. I speak to my daughter as a person. I respect her wishes and set healthy boundaries. I let her explore, fall down and experience life, but I'm also there to keep a watchful eye over her. Who I am for my daughter is vulnerable, open, truthful and fun. I practice letting her discover life on her own terms. All you can do as a parent is be the best version of yourself every day and lead by example. If your life is working, all your child can see is a happy and healthy parent who is engaged in their life. Perhaps your life isn't working? It doesn't matter. It's all about who you're being for them. Your child is a pure and loving soul who loves you unconditionally. Let them show you who you really are in amongst all that life throws your way. The pure love they exhibit is a healthy reminder when you have forgotten what life is really all about.

Challenges will arise as your child grows. It is inevitable that your child will shift and change over the years. They will form their own opinions, they will rebel, they will create their own stories, resentments can show up and they may disconnect or pull away from you. In those instances, how do you deal with that? Ultimately, it's your choice. It goes back to what kind of parent you want to be. You can always address any issues that may arise. In my opinion, it's best to talk things out. Don't avoid it. Don't let it build up. You are always in control as to how you handle your life. Your kids most likely want to share with you and sometimes there is a breakdown. Life throws so much at us, we have to check in and make sure our loved ones know that we are there and that we love them. We can get caught up in work or obligations that take our attention away from what matters. It's a healthy practice to get grounded and balanced to make sure we are here, present and not distracted. Being an absent parent can be a huge problem for children. This is particularly an issue in partnerships or marriages that have ended in divorce or separation. Don't let your kids feel like it is their fault or that you don't love them. Be transparent and open.

On the other hand, it can all be a positive experience where we raise our kids and it's a blissful and smooth existence. Our kids can be easy, low maintenance and chill. Childhood doesn't have to be tough or dramatic but this chapter is designed to have you take a look as to who you are in the midst of all of it. What kind of conversations are you having with yourself and with your kids? What actions are you taking as a parent? It shouldn't be a game to win but a way to be that inspires your children to strive and thrive in life. It really is that simple. At the end of the day, don't you want to give your kids the best possible everything that you are so they can have an **EPIC** and **AMAZING** life? So, do that. Don't let excuses, being tired, overwhelmed or distracted get in the way.

BE AMAZING!!

Let's do inventory. How are you doing in the realm of parenthood? Are you being the best example you can be? If not, ask yourself why? The coolest benefit is to your kids. They get to see and have the best possible **YOU** there is. How awesome is that? Get in action and make some positive changes. It's not that difficult. You'll have to do some work but the payoff is that you upgrade your life and your happiness. You confront the issue that is stopping you, acknowledge that it is a problem and do something about it. The biggest border to us breaking through to what and who we want to truly be is, **ACTION**. Action changes everything. So, take action. **NOW**. Not tomorrow. **NOW**. Waste not one second overthinking what is possible. You know in your heart you can always step your game up. We all have it in us. Do it for yourself and your kids. Make a splash and have some **FUN**.

CHAPTER 7
Co-Workers

Our relationship to our co-workers really speaks volumes as to who we are and how we perceive ourselves. I absolutely love this topic because it is the source of a lot of our breakdowns and issues with competitiveness in life. It also is a place where we are inspired to grow and challenge ourselves to do and be better. If we can put out finger on it and pinpoint where it all comes from, we can then create freedom around it.

The workplace. The place we often define ourselves by when it comes to our achievements in life.

We choose a career or job that requires a specific skill set that we work on mastering to have the best possible outcome. We get diplomas, certifications, degrees and all types of credentials to get us in the door of our "Dream Job". The question is, are you really doing what you dreamt of? Or are you settling for something that doesn't truly fulfill what makes you HAPPY and what lights you up?

The workplace commonly tends to be an ego-driven, 'I can do better than you' kind of environment where we push forward and fight daily to achieve certain goals and rankings. All of it based out of attaining some title or position that pays us more, gives us more to do and can sometimes put more stress on us. Why do we do this to ourselves? Social conditioning has definitely played a part in designing why it goes that way, worldwide. Most societies do it regardless of race, creed or color. It's a game of sorts to win and have all the toys and all of the trophies. But why? You have to have to ask yourself. What's my "Why"?

So, what's your relationship to your co-workers? Are you friendly and open? Do you keep to yourself? Are you a team player or the leader of the pack? More importantly, what actions do you take daily to build and foster these relationships? Are you giving it your all or are you just sliding by? Or are you somewhere in between? These are some of the inquiries you should ask yourself at this very moment. Where do you land in this conversation? Be truthful. That will help you uncover some things you may have avoided looking at.

It's a healthy place to start by looking right now and being fully honest with yourself about how life is for you when it comes to work. It's where you expend most of your effort of a daily basis. You are a part of a larger contribution and what you bring to the table matters. Taking stock of what you are within your work environment is important. Be wary of bringing any work upsets home with you. This is very common. Leave work at work. Be present to your life outside of work. Your job is something that you do to give you the lifestyle that you want – so honor your life. Don't impact your personal relationships because of stress related to work issues.

There is having a boss or being the boss. Bosses can be AMAZING, but they can also be just awful. If you are a person-in-charge, a boss, how are you treating your employees? Are you cold and callous? Or warm and welcoming? Check in with yourself to see where you are within this spectrum. They are your support team and without them, your world wouldn't work. It really is that simple. Be aware of how you carry yourself, the words you say and the actions you take. Why not create the most AMAZING environment that you can. Everyone wins in this scenario.

If you have a boss, how is your relationship to them? Is it working? Are there open lines of communication? Or is it stifled and uncomfortable? Wherever it's at, you are responsible for your part in it. You choose who you are about it and how you operate. They are who they are and all you can do is be GREAT at what you do. You cannot change them or tell them what to do. You can, however, create a clear and clean relationship to them to have a harmonious work place.

A powerful place to stand is, "what is yours is yours, and no-one can take that away from you". My mother said that to me years ago and it resonated with me.

Do the work. Be a great person. Build your profile within your work place, whatever that may be for you and SHINE. You will most likely inspire others to be greater as well. You CAN have a peaceful and beautiful relationship with your fellow workmates. It is totally up to you. You define you. You are the source of how it goes.

CHAPTER 8
Friends

I purposely put this chapter last because this is one of the most common areas in our life that matters to us most. Friends. These are the people who we CHOOSE in life to be by our side. The people we trust with our lives, dreams, secrets and spend tons of social time with. We, at a very early age in life discover what it is to have a 'friend'. It is someone you confide in, have fun with, and also create memories with. How awesome is that? You choose someone to be intimate, open and close with that you build a special bond with.

What is your definition of a friend? For me, a friend is someone that I share everything with, someone that I enjoy good times with and can rely on in the bad times, someone that holds me to the best version of myself and brings happiness and joy to my life. Friends are like family in certain instances. Friends are the family that we choose, not the ones we are given.

My point is, we go tend to go deeper with our friends sometimes than we do with our family. We let them in, we trust them. We share with them our greatest achievements and our biggest failures. I feel like friends are the 'gatekeepers' of the most intimate details of our lives.

Unfortunately, sometimes friendships fall apart. They fall apart because of insecurities, jealousies, unsaid expectations or a lack of communication. Sometimes we just grow apart. We don't say what we really want. We are afraid to be honest with what we need in our friendships. We hold back and don't clean up any messes we have made. We drop the ball and take no responsibility for it. All of those things can be contributing factors to friendships becoming toxic.

It is a sad reality but not everyone we meet and call "friends" have the best of intentions. There are many kinds of people out there. Chances are, in your lifetime your paths may cross with negative people. Our job in these moments is to be clear about who and want you want in your life. Never settle for less than AMAZING friendships. That's the point. Don't allow for people who steal your light and abuse your kindness. Allow for beauty and love in your world. It is a way more fulfilling place to operate from when that surrounds you.

Look at the closest people in your circle. They are a reflection of who you show up to BE in the world. It's just a simple truth. The mirror doesn't lie. You choose your circles and they choose you. If all of your friends are up to AMAZING things, you most likely are as well. If you are surrounded by people not living fully in their power, you are affected as well.

Here's a practice. Take notice of your friendships.

Are they holding you up to your best version of yourself?

Do they call you out and challenge you to grow?

Or, are they letting you slide and not be the best YOU possible?

Are they not holding you accountable for your dreams and goals being achieved?

Me personally, I keep friends in my life that inspire and challenge me, call me out on my shit, support and love me, and are just AMAZING human beings. They are up to something in life and so am I. Like attracts like. Your vibe attracts your tribe. It truly isn't hard to be UNSTOPPABLE. You just have to choose it.

Take a real hard look and see where you don't have people like that around you. Why? Why would you let yourself not be the greatest YOU that you can be? What is missing for you? If you can dig deep and find it, you can let it go. It isn't an easy practice but it is a powerful one. It involves forgiveness of SELF, LOVE from deep down and a willingness to have the life you really want. It's right here and right now. It's your journey and it's always been up to us to action it. Stop waiting and make it real today. As in NOW.

Let's ramp up your intimate friendships and cut out anything that isn't ridiculously delicious and juicy. These things are possible. You just have to confront certain realities that you have let become a part of your life. Time to face them, have the uncomfortable conversations and complete them. If you don't, life will continue to remain the same. That's fine, but it won't be AMAZING. You want to start getting out of the habit of letting things just fall by the wayside. You want to take responsibility for how your life looks and how you show up as a friend. Friendships are priceless. They are a choice. Choose wisely, be honest and make them INSANELY EXTRAORDINARY.

It's time to get to work and upgrade your friendships beyond where they have ever been. Take action. Tell the people that you love, you love them. Simple. Honor that. Today is a gift and let go of any past conversations that limit the amount of love that can be added. Add it. There is no such thing as "too much love".

Create profound friendships that can last a lifetime and watch how your life pans out.

Result

The intention of this book is to awaken your awareness as to how you treat your relationships. How you operate, the actions you take, the perceptions you have. I want to give you access to looking at it all candidly and honestly. To shift or change how you are being within them. To clean up anything that doesn't work for you. Something you may have wanted to do for a while but just allowed a circumstance or reason to stop you. Uncovering the issues that may lay beneath, that we choose to ignore, like the 'Elephant in the Room' can be freeing. When you create relationships from a place of love, it stands a chance to only be that. You **CAN** have **AMAZING** relationships in all areas of your life. You just have to want it and take actions consistent with that.

We do create different versions of ourselves to "survive" our lives. I say, let's **STOP** that and be our full authentic **SELF** with everyone. That's the goal. Unleashed, unapologetic, and just plain **AWESOME**!

Remember, when you get stuck, use The Relationship Tool to get straight to the source of the issue. It will make a difference.

Now go out and **HAVE AMAZING RELATIONSHIPS**.

ABOUT THE AUTHOR

Born in Brooklyn, NY to immigrant parents from Panama & Aruba, Shawn Antonio was raised in New York, Panama and Florida. Shawn now resides in Los Angeles with his Australian wife and young family. A trained dancer, Shawn spent the early part of his career running a dance company after deciding that a degree in medicine was not for him. After relocating to Los Angeles in his early 20's, Shawn worked briefly in reality television casting before going on to become one of Hollywood's most

Photo Credit: Alicia Antonio

respected and well known event promoters for over 16 years. In that time, Shawn has met millions of people. His ability to remember people and places is unmatched. Shawn's enthusiasm for life and boundless happiness is electric and infectious. Shawn has always been passionate about advocating for people and has spent many years on his own self improvement and personal growth. Some of the people who have inspired him are Paolo Coelho, Mahatma Gandhi, Mark Twain, Albert Einstein, Dale Carnegie, David Bowie, Martin Luther King Jr. and many others who drew outside the lines and truly changed the world. Shawn has inspired and guided thousands of people in his life, and felt the time was right to start writing his own books. Shawn is passionate about photography and travel, and his favorite destination is Egypt. Shawn speaks fluent Spanish and English.

Shawn is the author of 'Be The Beast You Are'.
This is the second book in Shawn's "Finding Your Fire" Series.
Look out for more titles coming soon.

Follow Shawn On Social Media!
@TheFireSeries
Facebook, Instagram, Twitter and Pinterest

ACKNOWLEDGMENTS

I want to thank everyone who stood by me as I created "Having Amazing Relationships". I was called to write this book to help guide people to having unbelievably **AMAZING** relationships. It is all possible. We often forget that. The gift that is this book was inspired by thousands of conversations I have had over the past few years. I realized there was a need for **LOVE** in the world that has been missing. I listened, I wrote, and I created this for all of the people living on this planet that simply want connection, love, and all the delicious morsels of what it is to be human that inspires us. Inspiration is **EVERYTHING**, in my opinion. So, **THANK YOU** to everyone who helped stop me in my tracks and told me "It's time. I need this in my life." So here it is.

Now go off and **HAVE... AMAZING... RELATIONSHIPS!!!**

Made in the
USA
Middletown, DE